Henry Edward Manning

Ireland

A Letter to Earl Grey

Henry Edward Manning

Ireland
A Letter to Earl Grey

ISBN/EAN: 9783744764230

Printed in Europe, USA, Canada, Australia, Japan

Cover: Foto ©Andreas Hilbeck / pixelio.de

More available books at **www.hansebooks.com**

IRELAND.

A LETTER

TO

EARL GREY.

BY ' ARCHBISHOP MANNING.

LONDON:

LONGMANS, GREEN, AND CO.

1868.

Price One Shilling.

MY LORD,

The justice with which you, as a Peer of Parliament, have always spoken of Ireland and of the Catholic Church, gives me confidence that you will bear with me if I express my mind upon these subjects. I venturē to address myself to you because your Lordship has long stood aloof from the two great parties in the State ; and in what I write, I desire to hold myself neutral between opposing sides. I make an appeal for justice, not to one side or the other, but to both. I have refrained from asking your Lordship's permission to inscribe your name upon this letter, because I wish you to be absolutely free from all responsibility as to any opinions I may express, and as to the prudence of my expressing them. That responsibility lies wholly on myself; and I have not hesitated to make this public declaration of my convictions, because it is evident that upon the future of Ireland hangs the future of the British Empire; and even the least may ask to be heard.

Let me anticipate a criticism by saying that I do not recognise any incompatibility between the sacred office I bear and the public treatment of these topics. It is not our belief that ecclesiastics cease to be citizens, or that anything affecting the common weal of our country is remote from our duty. This alone would suffice for my justification; but I may offer also other pleas for speaking publicly on subjects affecting Ireland. As an Englishman, I can speak to Englishmen without suspicion of a national bias, or, rather, with the national bias on the side of England. I may at least claim to be impartial. Again, the duties of many years, and the work of every day, have brought me into such direct and intimate contact with Ireland and the Irish people that I cannot be mistaken as to the gravity of the present crisis. I do not believe that it can be overrated. It is the disposition to underrate it, and the readiness to relapse into an untimely reassurance at every momentary lull of public anxiety, which fills me with most fear. It is true that we have had times of greater violence, and of more immediate dangers, than now threaten us; more fearful atrocities, both against the law and by the law, have been perpetrated, of which your Lordship has full memory; but there never yet was a moment in which such wide-spread and irresistible powers of change were in action upon the union of Great Britain and Ireland. It is enough to refer to the international organisations which unite Ireland to the continent of Europe, and to the intimate and vital bond which links Ireland to America. This is of a graver, deeper, mightier, and more permanent cha- racter than the risings of 1798 or of 1803. It is gradually assimilating and changing an integral part of the United Kingdom into a type which will hardly combine with ours, or consolidate the unity of these realms.

And now, my Lord, the subjects on which I will take the liberty to speak are, in my belief, still within

·the power of Parliament to control. · But the power of controlling them is becoming less and less as they are continually postponed. They may all be summed. up in two general heads, Religious Equality, and an equitable Land-law.

There is, however, one preliminary step to the pacification of Ireland, so easy in itself that we shall be gravely responsible if we do not at once take it; namely, that we in England should govern ourselves when we speak of Ireland, as we should expect Irishmen to govern themselves when they speak of us.' Nay, I will further say that the memory of the last three hundred years ought to make us all the more watchful, as those three centuries of suffering have made them all the more sensitive. I do not think Englishmen are enough aware of the harm some among us do by a contemptuous, satirical, disrespectful, defiant language in speaking of Ireland and the Irish people. A manly, generous, respectful tone would soon dispose many wounds to heal kindly which are kept open and fester rankly.

Your Lordship's treatment of these subjects has always been distinguished by a respectful and sympathetic manner towards Ireland: but I have been at a loss to conceive what certain of our public writers could hope to effect by the cynical, sarcastic disdain with which they treat that noble-hearted people. One of the most recent and melancholy examples of this, which I must call a public crime, may be found in the last article of the January number of the *Quarterly Review.* In that article, a writer of no ordinary abilities has exhibited, I hope as a warning to us all, how bitter, narrow, and unjust the spirit of party can make even a powerful mind. I call this a public crime, because it does more to create bad blood between the two countries than even graver wrongs. The grievances of a people may produce discontent, but a tone of imperial contempt goads high-spirited men to madness.

What is to be thought of an author's fairness who can deliberately write as follows: * 'As regards the Irish Church, for instance, a large majority of the representatives of Ireland are in favour of retaining it, and yet its destruction is constantly put forward as the means of appeasing Irish discontent?'

Does this 'large majority' of Protestant members, returned by Protestant influence, represent the views of the Irish Catholic people as to the advantages of maintaining a Protestant Establishment over their heads? If so, how is it that the remaining thirty Irish, but Catholic, members are, to a man, against it? Does Ireland speak by the majority or by the minority? The majority of the Irish members represent the minority of the Irish people. Lord Aberdeen's 'conundrum' is here proposed in a still more paradoxical form. So long as the majority of the Irish members are in favour of maintaining the Protestant Establishment, the majority of the Irish people is not represented. Is not this enough to explain and to justify popular discontent?

Again †—' So long as any considerable body of Irishmen seize greedily on every opportunity of parading their undying, irreconcilable hostility to

* P. 262. † P. 264.

the English connection; so long as we are to be opposed and thwarted—not because we are wrong, not because we are tyrannical, not because we are unjust, but because we are Englishmen—we must, on the simplest and plainest principles of self-defence, endeavour to satisfy and retain on our side that portion of the community that is friendly to British connection.'

Why should Englishmen be thwarted in Ireland, and why should English rule be thought 'wrong,' ' tyrannical,' ' unjust?' This is the evil to be removed. It is both easy and politic for the wrongdoer to proclaim oblivion of the past; but the sufferer of wrong can hardly be expected to be so pliant and forgetful. To our own hurt, we have made the English name hateful in the past, and we must bear the penalty till we have repaired the wrong—' Delicta majorum immeritus lues.' But is it not a reiteration of hard-hearted and hard-faced wrong to affect the manner of an innocent and injured party? Such a tone makes us partakers in the guilt of the past. To deny the justice of the prejudice attaching to us is to deny the injustice of the acts which caused it. We thereby justify the animosity of which we complain.

Again—' Whatsoever be the merits of land reform or of church destruction, they have nothing to do with Fenianism.' Has Fenianism any other cause than animosity against England? Has that animosity nothing to do with the three confiscations of almost every acre of land in Ireland, and the folly of striving for three hundred years to force the Reformation on a Catholic people?

Once more—' It has been the pleasure of Ireland to pass upon herself a sentence of perpetual poverty.' Did Ireland suicidally strip itself of all its lands, reduce itself to mud cabins, potato-diet and evictions, fever and famine? Would this have been the state of Ireland if it had been left to mature its own social order and civilisation as England, Scotland, France, and Spain? Who checked its agriculture, its cattle trade, its fisheries, and its manufactures, by Acts of Parliament? If poverty was ever inflicted by one nation on another, it has been inflicted on Ireland by England.

One more example—' As for laws and administration, Ireland is on the same footing with England; and where there is a difference, Ireland will be found to be better cared for than England.' Let the endowments of the Church of England be transferred to the English Catholic bishops and clergy; let the Anglican archbishops and bishops be liable to fine for assuming their ecclesiastical titles; let the land in England be held by absentee Irish landlords by title of past confiscations, and let their soil be tilled by tenants at will who may at any hour be evicted, and I shall then think that Ireland and England are on the same footing. There is yet one thing wanting. Let some Irish statesman reproach the English for their unreasoning and unrelenting animosity, their self-chosen poverty, their insensibility of the dignity and benefits of being thus treated by a superior race. But, my Lord, enough of this; which can have no other effect than to heat, blind, and distort the minds of men on both sides, and to come like Erinnys between the contending hosts to drive them to madness and mutual destruction.

There is, however, one last point in which, as the writer condescends to reason, I will ask leave to meet him in detail.

We are told that Ireland has one, and one only, grievance—not that its lands were confiscated; not that the heirs of old estates are now day labourers upon them ; not that its people have died by hundreds and by thousands, or have been driven away .by millions; not that its sacred revenues, its old parish churches, its cathedrals, dear for the memory of its saints and forefathers, have been taken away : all these things are as nothing. But there is one great grievance. The Irish people have to pay for their own religion. We have here the measure of this writer's breadth. Such is the knowledge, discernment, experience, compass, and trustworthiness of the guide who professes to teach the Imperial Parliament its duties towards Ireland, and Ireland its true condition.

Bear with me, my Lord, while I draw out to the full this new portentous wrong. To pay our own clergy is a grievance not to be found, I suppose, in England or Scotland. Why, half the people of England are Dissenters, and half the people of Scotland are Free-Kirk men. They all alike pay their own ministers. But, then, nobody wishes to detach them from their flocks, or their flocks from them ; or to buy their influence, or to destroy it, as of men that have been bought. We are further told : ' No position can be more cruel or painful than that of a Roman Catholic priest in Ireland really anxious to do his duty to his flock as a good pastor and to the State as a good citizen. He must live on their contributions ; they love him because they benefit him, and he must be no little of "a demagogue." He dare not appear loyal.' ' He is of the people,' and not only leads, ' but is led by sympathy, by the desire of popularity, and, it must be admitted, by pecuniary interest.' ' Few men can come out of such an ordeal without some loss of self-respect ;' 'some compliances ;' ' some "economies" of truth which they cannot look back upon without regret, and perhaps shame.' ' When we reflect on the vast power possessed by the priest,' ' we cannot sufficiently regret that the Government' 'has not drawn' them ' within the circle of its legitimate influence.' ' We cannot afford' to increase their ' influence by fixing upon the people the duty of maintaining ' their clergy ' side by side with the Episcopalian and Protestant Establishments,' &c. In plain English: We must pay them, but we must make the people believe that we do so solely to relieve them of their only grievance. We must get them in hand like the ministers of the Establishment, and so lessen their power over their flocks.

Do you now wonder, my Lord, that the Catholic clergy spurn the stipends of the English Government, and that the Catholic people of Ireland have a joy and pride in fulfilling the precept of the Apostle in maintaining their pastors? I thank the writer in the *Quarterly.* There is no danger of mistake in this matter.

But even this is not all. As if this professed compassion for the Irish people, oppressed by the grievance of giving gladly to their pastors, were not transparent enough, the writer goes on to add precautions against two dangers, namely, that the priests may refuse to take the Government pay, and that the people may persevere in giving to them. To effect these necessary precautions, the writer gives two counsels: The one: ' The salary should be paid into a bank ; ' and ' made seizable in execution for debt:' The other: ' Care must be taken to make known to the peasantry of Ireland that the State has taken upon itself the maintenance of the Roman Catholic clergy.' This done, ' We think that a priest questing for his support would meet with but little success,' &c. Bear with me, my Lord, if I translate this also into plain English : ' The priests are a greedy lot. They refuse the State money against their will. They are dying for it. All they want is a shadow of excuse. Pay it to their account in the bank. This will be enough for most of them. If any appear to hold out, make it seizable for debt. Let their butchers and bakers seize it. They will have touched the Queen's money, at least in kind. They could not go back if they would, and we know well enough, that they would not go back if they could. But they must affect to be above being paid. Give the man excuse, and they will take it fast enough.' My Lord, the Catholic priesthood of Ireland and of England will not fail to appreciate this exalted estimate of their sincerity, and the refined skill of this plot against their independence. For the other counsel, let all public men be well assured that, when the proclamation is made to the Irish people that the State has endeavoured to buy their pastors, there are no men living who will rise in greater indignation than the peasantry of Ireland. Without 'questing,' every priest in Ireland would find the free-will offerings of his people to be doubled: to let all men know that it is neither by questing nor by constraint, nor by undue influence, spiritual or personal, but for the love of God and of His Church, of their own souls, and of the souls of their children; and, I will be bold enough to add, for the love of their priests—their faithful, warm-hearted, unwearied friends, guardians, and guides in life and in death—that the Catholic people in Ireland, and the Catholic Irish in England, in Canada, in Australia, in the United States, throughout the world, joyfully, gratefully, generously, with filial love, cherish and support their clergy. The love of a Catholic Irishman for his priest is known only to those who have the happiness to labour among them. I can bear witness, and the Catholic clergy of England will bear witness with me, that no questing, or shearing, or spiritual terrorism, would be possible — if we were capable of an offence so base and hateful —and that such coercion is as needless as it would be impossible. There can hardly be found in Great Britain a population poorer than those who are driven by poverty from Ireland, and in England can hardly find employment except in the lowest forms of industry. Nevertheless, in all parts of England the same spirit of generosity and of piety, in everything which relates to the Church and the clergy, is to be found. The Irish people love both, because they know that no human power and no worldly interest separates their Church and their clergy from themselves. This independence is the pledge that they have a sole and exclusive right in both. To a State-paid Church and clergy the Catholics in England and Ireland would give neither their money nor their hearts.

I cannot but be sorry, my Lord, to read in a late Pamphlet a reference to supposed levies and exactions of priests upon their people. Such things here and there may have happened, for what nation is without its evils? but this is no sample of the Irish priesthood. Major O'Reilly, than whom few men better knew Ireland, estimates the outlay on churches, schools, convents, and other charitable institutions in Ireland since 1800 at 5,500,000*l*. Mr. Maguire, in his book on ' The Irish in America,' gives examples of the same Christian generosity in our North American colonies, and throughout the United States. The cathedral in the City of St. John's, Newfoundland, was built by them at a cost of 120,000*l*. The same profuse devotion to their faith is to be found wheresoever they are. The grandest cathedrals of these days have been raised by their alms.

But proofs are endless. Only let English statesmen once for all lay aside the illusion that the people of Ireland give because they are coerced; or that they would accept the relief of a State payment for their clergy; or that their clergy would acknowledge the account to which the counsel of Achitophel has carried the money to ensnare them. Both clergy and people would rather hunger and thirst together than dissolve the bond of Christian charity and Christian confidence which binds them indissolubly to each other.

The writer in the *Quarterly* must forgive me if I wrong him, but his quotation from Sydney Smith reveals the source of his inspiration. This scheme of

State policy is a plagiarism, but the humour of the original has evaporated. ' The first thing to be done is to pay the priests, and after a little while they will take the money. One man wants to repair his cottage; another wants a buggy; a third cannot shut his eyes to the dilapidation of a cassock. The draft is payable at sight in Dublin, or by agents in the next market town, dependant upon the commission in Dublin. The housekeeper of the holy man is importunate for money, and if it be not procured by drawing for the salary, it must be extorted by curses and comminations from the ragged worshippers slowly, sorrowfully, and sadly. There will be some opposition at first, but the facility of getting the salary without the violence they are now forced to use, and the difficulties to which they are exposed in procuring the payment of those emoluments to which they are fairly entitled, will, in the end, overcome all obstacles. And if it do not succeed, what harm is done by the attempt?' 'The Roman Catholic priest could not refuse to draw his salary from the State without incurring the indignation of his flock. Why are you to come upon us for all this money when you can ride over to Sligo or Belfast and draw a draft upon Government for the amount? It is not easy to give a satisfactory answer to this to a shrewd man who is starving to death.'* The Irish people, both clergy and laity, well knew the genial and friendly humour of the Canon of St. Paul's, and laughed heartily at both him and his scheme, but they will read with a very different heart this old joke in the earnest bitterness of the plagiarist.

* Works of Sydney Smith, p. 681. Longmans, 1850.

It is a relief to turn to the words of a statesman who knew Ireland better: ' My inference from the matter is this, that, if the Castle-ascendency could bribe the whole body of the Roman Catholic clergy (a thing not very likely) into a treacherous conduct towards three millions of their laity—that not anything else would result from it than this, that they would never attend on the ministry of one of these corrupt and silly creatures. They would call them the *Castleick* clergy. They would have other priests; and though this might add a little to the confusions of the country and to the public expenses (the great object next to the job, to which they have reduced the public interests), they might be sure it would not lessen by one the number of those who contend for justice on the tenour of the good old common law of England, and the principles of the English constitution.' *

A very estimable member of the House of Commons said to me the other day: ' The priest in Ireland is our enemy. I wish to have him as my friend.' The priests will be so when we deal justly with their faith and with their people, and cease to treat them as if they could be bought.

Let me now take leave of the Quarterly Reviewer and his one only grievance amidst the exuberant prosperities of thankless and intractable Ireland.

We ought to respect the sensitiveness kept alive in a noble people by the memory of religious persecutions which England desires to erase from its records, and by natural resentments kindled by

* Letter of Edmund Burke to his son Richard Burke, June 1792. Correspondence, vol. iv. p. 15.

repeated and terrible confiscations. I am not now
about to recite the wrongs of the past, nor to rekindle
the fires which have been, happily, dying down. We
shall rejoice to forget the past, but on one condition.
Let us hear no more of 'sentimental grievances,' no
heartless assertions that Ireland has now nothing to
complain of; that the reign of Astrea is supreme in
Ireland; that the Irish do not know their own golden
prosperity, created by English and Scottish industry,
while they will do nothing but saunter and look on
with folded arms. Let us have no more of this unjust and dangerous language, and we shall carefully
refrain from raking up the embers of history. It
needs little stirring to raise a flame. We Englishmen
can be cool and calm in this matter, but we must not
forget that the accumulated animosity of the past is
born in the blood of Irishmen. My surprise is not
that they control it so little, but that they control it
so much. The social and political inequalities, the
religious persecutions, and the cruel confiscations of
the past, might be more easily forgotten if they were
not still embodied, visibly and grievously before their
eyes, in the ascendency of the Protestant Establishment and of a minority. This is the recapitulation
and representative of the policy of Elizabeth, James,
and Cromwell, still living, powerful, and dominant.
I will not, however, revive these bitter topics. We
Englishmen ought, indeed, to be calm and to control
ourselves. But can we wonder if no Irishman be as
cold-blooded as we are? It is this unreasonable, I
was about to say this unnatural, mood of mind which
renders the language of Englishmen so irritating to

Ireland. 'As vinegar upon nitre, so is one that singeth songs to a heavy heart.' Such are the hymns to Irish prosperity in the ears of a population a century behind the national maturity which is their right. Society which springs from the soil, and forms itself by the tillage of the land, training its people to thrift and industry, and unfolding its steady growth in homes, hamlets, villages, towns, and cities—ripening by centuries of time, and binding all orders and inequalities of rich and poor, master and servant, together in mutual dependence, mutual justice, mutual charity, making even the idle to be thrifty, and the powerful to be compassionate, this growth of human happiness and social order, which in England and Scotland is so symmetrical and mature, in Ireland has been checked at the root. The centuries which have ripened England and Scotland with flower and fruit have swept over Ireland in withering and desolation. We are beginning in the nineteenth century to undo the miseries of the seventeenth and the eighteenth. But let us not excuse ourselves by alleging the faults of national character. If our Irish brethren have faults, they are, for the most part, what England has made them. We Englishmen, with a like treatment, would have been the same.

It would be blindness not to see, and madness to deny, that we have entered into another crisis in the relations of England and Ireland, of which '98, '28, and '48 were precursors. In '98, '28, '48, the revolutionary movements of the Continent powerfully acted upon this country. In 1868, not the Continent only but America is in direct and hostile action upon all the elements of disorder, and, what is more dangerous, upon all the causes of just discontent in this country. My Lord, if just discontent were removed, disorder would bring no danger. The public moral sense of the United Kingdom would reduce all disorders to submission, if justice were on our side. I do not deny that for the last fifty years the Legislature of this country has desired to deal justly with Ireland. But I must altogether deny that the Legislature has as yet done its duty by Ireland, or that the causes of just discontent in Ireland have been removed.

So much for the first reason of disunion among us. Let us now go on to the other causes of, what I must persist in calling, just discontent.

So long as there exists upon the statute-book any penal enactment against the Catholic religion; so long as the Catholic people of Ireland are deprived of a *bona fide* Catholic education; so long as a Protestant Church Establishment is maintained by law over the face of Catholic Ireland; and so long as the people of Ireland fail to derive from the land such a subsistence as the labourers and farmers of England and Scotland derive from the soil: there must be a just discontent, which will be the misery of Ireland and the danger of England.

Here, then, are four distinct heads of a discontent which is just. Two of them, as I venture to say, may be removed to-morrow if Parliament have the will to do it; two of them are more complex and difficult, and may require time for eradication. But even these can be removed, and, if the peace and welfare of these kingdoms are to be preserved, they must be removed, and that as speedily as can be.

The two remedies which can at once be applied are these: The first, an Act of Parliament, summed up in one clause, which would recite and repeal all penal enactments against the Catholic Church and religion still lingering in the statutes of these realms. No people can see without resentment the stigma of legal ignominy branded upon their pastors and their faith; no government can command the confidence of those whom it deliberately wounds in that which is dearer than life itself. These penal statutes gall, irritate, outrage the noblest and deepest instincts of pastor and people. And what has the Government of our country gained by such fatal laws? Has it repressed Catholicism? has it propagated the Reformation? What has it produced but the profound mistrust and resentment in a whole people, which is now one of our chief dangers, because it elevates all other griefs with the higher character of religious persecution? The day is past for legislation against religious faith: it is two hundred years after date. If Ireland is to be justly pacified, the Church of the people must be placed upon the perfect equality which it enjoys in Canada and Australia. So long as Parliament shall legislate for Catholic Ireland in compliance with the religious prejudices of England and Scotland, Ireland will have a just cause of discontent. Is it consistent with the dignity of the Imperial Parliament to pass laws which the Christian world ignores? We cannot legislate for the Gulf Stream, or change the course of the trade winds, by Act of Parliament. If these statutes were consistent with wisdom when the framers believed that they could be executed, they are no longer wise when time has fought against them and shown them to be powerless.

The other measure of pressing importance to Ireland, which may be passed at once if any Government have the will to do so, is such a modification of the National Education Board as shall make the existing schools *bona.fide* denominational schools of the Catholic and of the Protestant populations respectively. It is a keen irony to call a system of education National where the religion of the nation may neither be taught nor exhibited in its schools. If the people of Ireland had been consulted at its foundation, it would never have come into existence. If they were polled now, it would not survive a day. It is not a national but a Government education, distasteful to almost the whole population of Ireland, to Catholics and to Protestants alike. Both would be glad to see it resolved into denominational education. It would promote peace, contentment, and good will, to give over the schools in each place to the majority, be it Catholic or Protestant. The Catholic minority would gladly provide its own Catholic school. The Protestant minority would be easily provided for out of the wealth of the Protestant clergy and landlords.

Let it be borne in mind that the National system in Ireland, though called a mixed one, is, to a great extent, not so in fact.

1. There are 2,454 schools, containing 373,756 Catholic children, with not a Protestant child.

2. There are 2,483 schools, having 321,641 Catholic children, with only 24,381 Protestant children.

That is, in 4,937—nearly 5,000—schools, with 695,397 Catholic children, there are no more than 24,381 Protestant.

Nevertheless, in these 4,937 schools, containing 965,397 Catholic children, it is not permitted to teach publicly the Catholic religion, to use Catholic books, or to put up a crucifix. This is no 'sentimental grievance,' but a real and grave interference, which paralyses the Catholic education of the Irish people. And yet they have as good right to their own national education as England or Scotland, and for the same reasons. The National system of England is Anglican, the National system of Scotland is Presbyterian, the National system of Ireland is not Catholic. Why should the National system of Ireland be deprived of its national religion? Even in England, the Catholic Church has its denominational schools. The Catholic Church in Ireland is deprived of them in deference to a small number of Protestants. The Catholic population in Ireland, as compared with the Protestant, is four to one. In three of the provinces, namely, Munster, Leinster, and Connaught, almost eight-tenths of the schools are exclusively Catholic. In the one province of Ulster alone are the schools to any extent mixed; many are exclusively Catholic: and even in Ulster the Catholics outnumber the Protestants. On what principle, then, of common justice can a Catholic denominational education be refused to the Catholic people in Ireland? In England it could not be refused to the Catholics in 1847, because the Protestants of England demanded it for themselves. In Ireland it was refused to the Catholics, and the whole education of Ireland was stripped of its Catholic character for the sake of a minority of Protestants, who were, in 1835, not even one-sixth of the population. And yet this system has not pleased even the Protestants. So strongly marked is the aversion of both Catholics and Protestants for this mixed education that, when they can separate, they do so. In Dublin, there are sixty National schools taught by Catholic teachers, containing 24,355 children on the roll. Of these, only six are Protestants, and four are Jews. But in parts of Ireland where there is no such alternative, a still greater grievance arises. It is shown by a Parliamentary return, obtained by Major O'Reilly, that in National schools of which Presbyterians have control, thousands of Catholic children are obliged to attend. In these schools they received religious instruction from Protestant masters, learned Protestant Catechisms, and read the Protestant version of the Bible.

Can we be surprised that the Irish people resent this as an injustice and as a penal enactment? The whole population in Ireland would rejoice in the resolution of the National system into *bona fide* denominational schools. The Protestants would be as thankful as the Catholics. What is gained by tying them together in an unwilling alliance, distasteful to Protestants, and penal upon Catholics? Surely Government has no need to create new Irish difficulties: nor to keep alive for a day, a grievance which might be taken away by Act of Parliament, as I have said, in one clause.

When the Irish ask for a Parliament in Dublin, they are reminded that it would reduce them from the dignity of an integral part of the mother country to the level of a colony. But England treats its colonies, in education as well as in religious equality, better than it treats Ireland. If the dignity of belonging to the mother country is to be purchased by the grievance of religious inequality, and of education stripped of the national religion, Ireland may be forgiven for asking for the portion of a daughter, and to be treated as a colony. The British Government has chartered and endowed colleges at Sydney and Melbourne, in Australia, and a Catholic University in Canada. But in Ireland the Catholic University has neither charter nor endowment. Three mixed colleges, which I must call by the Christian name Sir Robert Inglis gave them— Godless—are offered to four millions of Catholics in Ireland; whilst the million of Protestants possess Trinity College, Dublin, endowed with 190,000 acres of land and a revenue of upwards of 30,000*l.* a year. These things the British Government has done for the Catholics of Canada, who are 1,200,000, and for the Catholics of Australia, who are some hundred thousands; but for the Catholic population of 4,500,000 in Ireland, neither charter nor endowment has been given. Is it strange that Ireland is not sufficiently sensible of the benefit of being called a part of the mother country? Above all, as it is not thus that the mother country treats itself.

I come now to the two other subjects which demand more time for their settlement. They are both, however, within the control of Parliament, and both lie deep in the discontent of Ireland.

The first is the Established Church. It is long since I have heard any man argue for it. The Quarterly Reviewer, indeed, calls it ' the garrison;' and that perhaps is the most and the best, perhaps also the worst, that friend and foe could say of it. England tried for a century to force Episcopacy upon Scotland. It has tried for three to force Protestantism upon Ireland. England had the timely wisdom to leave Scotland to its own religion. Let it have the tardy wisdom to leave Ireland to its faith. It may as well try to change the saltness of the sea as to make the Irish people Protestants. They have multiplied from the remnant of Connaught to a people which outnumbers fourfold their Protestant brethren, and overspreads in its dispersion the colonies of Great Britain and the United States of America. The dream of conversion is long since dispelled for ever. There does not remain a shadow of reason or of justice for the hostile Church which for three hundred years has overspread the whole Catholic people of Ireland. Nay, more than this : it has become a danger to the Empire, and a reproach to England in the eyes of the whole Christian and civilised world.*

* Mr. Burke did not consider the Protestant Establishment in Ireland ' a sentimental grievance.' His language in 1792 is happily, to a great extent, inapplicable to these times. But the following words are valuable, as showing that, in his judgment, it was the religious ascendancy which produced and perpetuated the miseries of Ireland :—

The bishops of Ireland assembled in October last year, and made a noble and Christian declaration. After affirming that the existence of a State Protestant Church spread all over Catholic Ireland is ' the fountain head of bitterness which poisons the relations of life, and estranges Protestants and Catholics, who ought to be an united people,' the document goes on to say that the bishops and clergy will never accept endowment at the hands of the State out of the property and revenues once the possession of the Catholic Church, but now held by the Protestant Establishment.

I do not pretend to represent those most reverend prelates, but I seem to see the highest and most self-evident reasons for this resolution.

First.—It is not difficult to imagine what would be the imputations heaped upon them if they had allowed the State to suppose that, in demanding the disendowment of the Establishment, they were willing to accept its revenues. A storm of popular abuse and of refined contempt would have pursued them as greedy, covetous, and grasping.

Secondly.—If the revenues of the Establishment were transferred to the Catholic Church, a cause of

---

' I can never persuade myself that anything in our Thirty-nine Articles which differs from their Articles is worth making three millions of people slaves, to secure its teaching at the public expense; and I think he must be a strange man, a strange Christian, and a strange Englishman, who would not rather see Ireland a free, flourishing, happy *Catholic* country, though not *one* Protestant existed in it, than an enslaved, beggared, insulted, degraded Catholic country, as it is, with some Protestants here and there scattered through it, for the purpose, not of instructing the people, but of rendering them miserable.'—*Letter of March* 23, 1792, *to Richard Burke, Jun.* Correspondence, vol. iii. p. 452.

deadly and intense heart-burning would at once spring up. The Protestants of Ireland would be excited to a sevenfold greater animosity against their Catholic fellow-subjects. A new and bitter hatred would have heated the furnace sevenfold. In this the bishops have consulted, not only as Christians, but as statesmen, for the peace of the country, and even for the welfare of their adversaries.

Thirdly.—In the last three centuries of its poverty, the Church in Ireland has been once more supplied by the Divine Providence with sufficient revenues. Once it possessed fixed endowments : now it is endowed with the free-will offerings of the people. Burke, in a letter to his son, had this in view when he described the Catholic Church in Ireland, some few points excepted, as ' an image of a primitive Catholic Church.' * They that serve the altar in Ireland live of the altar. The highest exercise of mutual charity is reciprocally manifested by the pastors and their flocks. The old Church property has been desecrated, a new endowment has been found. When an old chalice has been stolen, a new one is consecrated. If

---

* 'I very much wish to see, before my death, an image of a primitive Christian Church. With little improvements, I think the Roman Catholic Church of Ireland very capable of exhibiting that state of things. I should not, by force or fraud, or rapine, have ever reduced them to their present state. God forbid ! But being in it, I conceive that much may be made of it, to the glory of religion, and the good of the State. If the other was willing to hear of any melioration, it might, without any strong perceivable change, be rendered much more useful. But prosperity is not apt to receive good lessons, nor always to give them ; re-baptism you won't allow, but truly it would not be amiss for the Christian world to be re-christened.' — *Letter to Rev. Dr. Hussey, February* 27, 1795. Correspondence, vol. iv. p. 284.

the old one were restored, as it has been desecrated,
melt it down, and give the silver to the poor. A
new one has been provided, the old one is no longer
needed. So with the old endowments. They belonged
once to God. They have been taken away, and He
has provided in another form for the service of His
Altar. They ought indeed to be restored: and let the
restitution be fully made. But let it be made to Him
in the hands of His poor. They are His representatives. Therefore it is that the bishops declare that,
' by appropriating the ecclesiastical property of Ireland for the benefit of the poor, the Legislature would
realise one of the purposes for which it was originally
destined, and to which it was applied in Catholic
times.' By this, the bishops do not mean that it
should be applied to relieve the landlords of the poor-
rates, or the Government of the cost of education, but
in other ways for which there is no provision.

There are many works of piety and charity much
needed in Ireland which would absorb much. The
rest would go direct to the poor if it were applied to
such a settlement of the land as would lift the families
of the poor by giving them an interest in the soil.

But the question of applying the proceeds, be it
easy or difficult of solution, in no way bears upon the
absolute duty of withdrawing from Catholic Ireland
the ubiquitous offence and challenge of a Protestant
Establishment in every diocese and in every parish,
where sometimes the whole population is exclusively
Catholic. Perfect religious equality, as in Canada
and Australia, is the sole way of peace and justice
between England and Ireland.

And now, my Lord, I will not shrink from venturing even upon the land question; because it is the chief and paramount condition on which the peace of Ireland depends. In comparison with this question, all others are light. It is the question of the people and of the poor; of social peace or agrarian war; of life or of death to millions. Until lately, we have been led to believe that no one could understand it. We have been persuaded by the confident assertions of men to shut our mouths before it, as if it had some special and infallible difficulty; as if it were a problem that statesmen could not unravel, of which political economists could render no account. Foreign nations are not of this opinion: they see no exceptional difficulty or complexity about it, and there are some general truths and governing axioms connected with it about which there can be no reasonable doubt. To these I shall confine myself, and they will be enough to show the inevitable necessity of legislation on the relation of the Irish people to the land.

I will begin, then, by affirming that there is a natural and divine law, anterior and superior to all human and civil law, by which every people has a right to live of the fruits of the soil on which they are born, and in which they are buried. This is a right older and higher than any personal right. It is the intrinsic right of the whole people and society, out of which all private rights to the soil and its fruits are created, and by which those created rights must always be controlled. A starving man commits no theft if he saves his life by eating of his neighbour's bread so much as is necessary for the support of his existence. The civil law yields before the higher jurisdiction of the divine, as the positive divine law yields before the natural law of God. Even the 'shewbread' might be eaten to save life. If at any time the civil laws shall so define the property of private persons as to damage the public weal, the supreme civil power has both the power and the duty so to modify those private rights as to reconcile them with the public good. No better example can be found than in the Act of Elizabeth, whereby the land in England was charged with the relief of the poor. The Law of Settlement is a modified right to the soil—a right to live on it and of it. The poor are joint owners of the usufruct. The land being a fixed quantity, and the people an extending quantity, it is inevitable that the preoccupation of the whole area of the country by a small number of landlords must have the effect of excluding or disinheriting the greater part of the people from all possession of the soil. The poor law, therefore, charged the general estate with a rent-charge for the younger children of the realm. Nothing can be conceived more just; and yet, when it was proposed in 1838 for Ireland, it was called 'confiscation.' For three hundred years, the landlords in England had clearly recognised it as a just law; Irish landlords resisted it as a violation of the rights of property. It is to be doubted if the land laws of England would have lasted till this date if the Act of Elizabeth had not made their exclusiveness tolerable to the mass of the people. Here, then, is a wise and just modification of private

rights by a higher law—'Salus populi suprema lex.'
It is a law as conservative as it is just. Without it,
where would be now the great estates of England?
The late Sir Robert Peel said to a friend, from whom
I heard it, that by the repeal of the corn laws he had
saved the landlords against their will. The same
will, I trust, be true of the land laws in Ireland.

I need not recite what all men know, that there is
no right of private property which is not modified,
not only by those higher laws, but also by a multitude
of positive enactments, based only on public utility.
What are the forced sales of all kinds of property,
even the most valuable to the owners, ancestral
estates, and cherished homes, if a line of railway be
required? In building our own dwelling-houses, we
are limited and controlled in endless ways, as to
frontages, and lights, and construction. We cannot
use our own land except under limitations which
take from its extent. We cannot do what we will
with our own. We cannot even let in the light of
heaven, which is *res nullius*, and therefore the uni-
versal property of all men, except under conditions
which protect our neighbour, not in life and limb,
but in convenience and comfort. We may not set up
mills or works upon a river which may cause the
stream to alter its course, and to damage our neighbour down the stream. We may not bank our own
side of the river so as to make it eat away the shore
of the opposite owner. Our whole law is full of
wise, equitable, merciful limitations upon the absolute right of private property. The notion that
we may do what we will with our own, that is, that

we have no limit to our use but our own will, is false every way, immoral, and contrary to all laws civil, natural, and divine. In the use and engagement of our private rights, we are subject to the public good. If we respect the public good, the Legislature has no need to intervene. If we use our extreme rights to our neighbour's hurt, the law will justly come in to protect him, and to limit our freedom. In England the traditions of centuries, the steady growth of our mature social order, the ripening of our agriculture and of our industry, the even distribution and increase of wealth, has reduced the relation of landlord and tenant to a fixed, though it be an unwritten, law, by which the rights of both are protected. There may be in England no need of land laws. Our land customs may be enforced in the courts, and thereby have the force of law. English landlords, as a rule, live on their estates. Their lands are their homes. English tenants are protected by the mightiest power that ever ruled a Christian country—a power which controls the Legislature, dictates the Laws, and guides even the sovereignty of the Crown—the force of a vigilant, watchful, ubiquitous, public opinion.

But in Ireland none of these things are so. In one-fourth of Ireland, there are land laws, or, rather, land customs, which protect the tenant. In three-fourths of Ireland, there are neither laws nor customs. The tenants are tenants at will. Over a vast proportion of Ireland, the landlords are absentees. The mitigating and restraining influences of the lords of the soil which, in England, and in every civilised country, do more to correct the excesses of agents, speculators, and traffickers, and to temper legal rights with equity and moderation, are hardly to be found. The substantial improvements upon farms, and the buildings necessary for agriculture, are made, not by the landlord, as in England, but by the tenant in Ireland. Is this to be found in any other country of Europe? The tenant has no security that his outlay is his own, or that he shall ever reap the benefit of it. Whatever goes into the soil, whatever is built upon it, 'fructificat domino.' The landlord may raise his rent at will, and give him notice to quit at will. The tenant at will may be put out for any cause; not only for nonpayment of rent, or waste of his land, or bad farming, or breach of covenant, if such can be supposed to exist, all of which would bear a colour of justice; but for the personal advantage of the landlord arising from the tenant's improvements; for political influence; for caprice, for any passing reason or no reason, assigned, or not assignable, which can arise in minds conscious of absolute and irresponsible power. This is an evil state. Absolute and irresponsible power is too great for man. Even supreme civil rulers do not possess it; but the rights of property, as they are claimed in Ireland, in respect to the amount of rent and the eviction of tenants, are absolute and irresponsible. The very term 'tenant at will' is there of dangerous sound. If the events which have passed in Ireland since 1810 had passed in England, the public opinion of this country would have imperiously compelled the Legislature to turn our land customs into Acts of Parliament. If any sensible proportion of the people of the English counties were to be seen moving down upon the Thames for embarkation to America, and dropping by the roadside from hunger and fever, and it had been heard by the wayside that they were 'tenants at will,' evicted for any cause whatsoever, the public opinion of the country would have risen to render impossible the repetition of such absolute and irresponsible exercise of legal rights. It would erect tribunals to judge between landlords and tenants; it would reduce to open and legal process the exercise of these imperial rights claimed by private citizens. If five millions, that is, a fourth of the English people, had either emigrated in a mass, by reason of discontent, misery, or eviction, or had died by fever and by famine since the year 1848, the whole land system of England would have been modified so as to render the return of such a national danger impossible for ever. But both these suppositions have been verified in Ireland.

Whole counties have been sensibly drained of their population; the public ways have been choked by departing trains of emigrants; one-fourth of the population of Ireland fled from it, or died of hunger and fever, and yet the Legislature still maintains the land laws under which these things are possible. Parliament did, indeed, fifteen years ago, solemnly recognise the right of tenants, but that recognition lies dead on the record. This, too, adds bitterness to those who suffer. Their right has been acknowledged, but its protection has for fifteen years been delayed. Of this, however, it will be better to speak hereafter. That I may not seem to use exaggeration, I will give one or two statements from an authority I cannot mistrust. In the year 1849, more than 50,000 evictions took place; more than 50,000 families were turned out of their dwellings without pity, and without refuge. ' If we assume that the evictions of one year, 1849, admitting it to be an exceptional one, represented a fifth of those which occurred in twenty years, our calculation would be below and not above the truth. Give only four individuals to each evicted family, and we have, on a moderate estimate, one million of human beings driven by force from their homes.'* This is softly called a ' clearance.' Mr. Butt, from whom I quote these statements, goes on to say: ' Let us estimate impartially—calmly, if we can—the character of these evictions. They were not the ordinary transactions in which the owner of property reclaims it from persons in whose hands he does not wish it to remain; they were in many instances clearances of estates, that is, the dispossession of a whole population from their ancestral homes. These people were cottiers, it is true. Their existence had become inconvenient to the great lord to whose ancestors Oliver Cromwell's grant had given the ownership of the land. From generation to generation, they and their forefathers had lived as cottiers upon that land under a system tolerated by law. The hope of gain, the dread of a poor-rate, the desire for large farms, had prompted the edict which commanded that the whole condition of life in an entire district shall be changed. By what name shall we call a wholesale extermination that followed such an edict as this? It

* Land Tenure in Ireland, by Isaac Butt, Esq. p. 34.

is vain to disguise it as the exercise of any right of civilised property.' *

The same author adds two other instances. 'I could tell of another estate, on which the landlord's agent has laid down the rule that, under no circumstances, shall two families be permitted to live in the same house. An aged widow invited a daughter, who had lost her husband, to take share of her house. For this crime, although occupying a respectable position, the mother of a Roman Catholic priest, she is actually evicted from a farm where she had lived for nearly fifty years. She is given her choice to leave that home, or send away her daughter.'

One other instance, and it is the last. 'A townland in one of the midland counties was inhabited by a prosperous and contented community. An estate of about five hundred acres was divided into thirteen farms; thirteen thriving families occupied the ground, a happy and contented tenantry, numbering thirteen families. They paid, as rent, the full value of their farms. They paid that rent punctually. The families of some had occupied, for centuries, the same farms. The industry of themselves and their forefathers had given fertility to the soil. Crime was unknown among them. Disputes with their landlord they had none.

' It suited the convenience of their landlord to sell his interest in this estate. The purchaser was buying it to traffic in it, and he believed it would be more marketable if it were freed from the incumbrance of human beings. To effectuate this object, the seller

---

* Land Tenure in Ireland, p. 34.

covenanted to clear the estate. The tenants who had paid up every penny of their rent, were all served with notice to quit; they were all evicted. Thirteen human habitations were levelled, the inmates turned out upon the world, reduced at once from comfort to absolute beggary. It so happened that, in this instance, the landlord adopted a course which enabled a jury to strain the law, and award these poor tenants ample compensation. But for the awkwardness with which the proceeding was carried out, it might all have been done without the power of any human tribunal to take cognisance of the wrong. An accidental blunder in the process put it in the power of a jury of landlords, by the damages they awarded, to mark their sense of the moral character of the act.' *

I doubt not, my Lord, that these things already are well known to you. But I believe they are unknown to the English people at large. I do not believe they would rest a day without crying out to be delivered from the shame of partaking, even by silence, in such atrocities. When a writer like Mr. Mill affirms that the conscience of Europe condemns us for our treatment of Ireland, there are critics among us who deride his words. But his words are measured and true. I have talked freely for many years with men of most countries in Europe. I have found everywhere a profound sympathy with Ireland, in no way flattering to England. Our insularity keeps these things from our ears, and we therefore soothe ourselves with the notion of our own superiority to other men. But such an abuse of the rights of property

* Land Tenure in Ireland, p. 40.

is without parallel, at least in this century, on the continent of Europe. Our self-respect should lead us to give up the illusion that our office in the civilised world is to 'teach the nations how to live.' We may learn of Prussia, France, Switzerland, and Tuscany, even of Canada and Prince Edward's Island, all of which are in advance of England in the solution of what is called the 'land question' in Ireland.

How is it to be expected that a people will be industrious who have no security that they will not be swept off the land they till? How will they improve it if they have no security that they shall retain the benefit of that improvement? How shall justice be done to the land unless it be improved by advancing cultivation? How shall cultivation advance if improvements be visited by a rise in the rent, and the increased rent be enforced by notice to quit? How shall the land so treated fail to breed famine and fever, and a people so harassed restrain themselves from a wild discontent and bitter retaliation? The same would be the state of England if custom, which is the 'mother of quietness,' and therefore of plenty, did not protect the tenant from arbitrary rents and arbitrary evictions.

It is sometimes over-boldly said that landlords in Ireland are not guilty of these abuses of extreme rights. If so, then they would not be in any way wronged if the Legislature, by statute, should make such abuses to be for ever impossible. The bare possibility of such acts of arbitrary power destroys confidence, and ought to be legally extinguished. What just landlord would complain if he were so limited by law as to be unable to commit three wrongs—first, the wrong of abusing his right by arbitrary eviction; secondly, by exacting an exorbitant rent; thirdly, by appropriating to his own use the improvements effected by the industry of his tenants? A merciful man would not only not resent such a law but would gladly preclude the possibility that any owner of land should blot the fair name of landlord, and embitter the hearts of men against his whole class by such injustice. It has been well said, ' A whole people must not hold their position in the country upon the chances of individual character. In a country like Ireland, to give the power of doing such things is to ensure that they will be done.' * And none would be more glad of such merciful laws as would prevent their being done than they who now mercifully use their arbitrary rights and refrain from doing them.

But it is not my intention to enter into any detailed plans or schemes for such a purpose. I do not pretend to draft a land bill, or even to give the heads. But anyone may lay down the principles which ought to govern this question, and may do so without hesitation, and upon the highest authority. In the year 1852, the Government of Lord Derby introduced a Bill affirming the great principle of equity, ' That the property created by the industry of the tenant belongs of right and in justice to himself, and that it is the duty of the Legislature to protect it by law.' †

This Bill was accepted and supported by the Government of Lord Aberdeen, which succeeded in 1853.

* Land Tenure in Ireland, p. 40.
† Ibid. p. 85.

It was supported by all the three great political parties
in the State. It was urged upon Parliament by the
first statesmen and lawyers of the day, by Lord Pal-
merston, Mr. Gladstone, Sir George Grey, Sir George
Lewis, by Sir Richard Bethell, Mr. Cairns, Mr. Napier,
Mr. Whiteside, now four of the highest authorities of the
law in Great Britain and Ireland. The Bill was passed
by large majorities, but never became law. In 1855,
it was revived in the House of Commons, and lost.
But majorities, though they make laws, cannot unmake
rights. The great right of equity, once so clearly seen
and so authoritatively enunciated, remains as a witness
of justice, and a warning of the danger which will never
pass away till justice be done. I say justice without
fear, because legal right is not always just. The highest
legal right is sometimes the greatest wrong. Human
law is but an imperfect expression of the natural
and divine right which is anterior and superior to all
legislation. There are axioms and principles which
restrain, modify, and suspend the action of law, and
become a higher law of supreme jurisdiction. What
is the High Court of Equity but a tribunal above
the law, dispensing justice often against the letter
of the law of which it may be truly said, ' The
letter killeth, the spirit giveth life ' ? And what
is the High Court of Parliament but a tribunal
higher even than the Court of Chancery ?—and to
this tribunal the Irish people come, as Sicily came
of old for redress of wrongs to the Imperial Senate.
Ireland prays that it may be declared by the Sovereign Justice of the Empire that the property in
the soil which the industry and enterprise of the tillers

and tenants of the soil have created, though by law it belongs to the landlord, nevertheless, by moral right, higher than all other law, belongs to those who have created it. Of this supreme right of natural and divine justice, it is, that they claim the protection of the highest tribunal of the realm. Scotland and England already possess this security by customs. Why should it be denied to Ireland? Where these customs exist, they ought to be made into law; where they do not exist, they ought by law to be created.

It may be thought that I have ventured to speak upon a subject which is beyond both my capacity and my duty. But I have done so from the profound conviction that the deepest and sorest cause of the discontent and unrest of Ireland is the land question. I am day by day in contact with an impoverished race driven from home by the land question. I see it daily in the destitution of my flock. The religious inequality does indeed keenly wound and excite the Irish people. Peace and good will can never reign in Ireland until every stigma is effaced from the Catholic Church and faith, and the galling injustice of religious inequality shall have been redressed. This, indeed, is true. But the 'Land Question,' as we call it, by a somewhat heartless euphemism, means hunger, thirst, nakedness, notice to quit, labour spent in vain, the toil of years seized upon, the breaking up of homes, the miseries, sicknesses, deaths, of parents, children, wives; the despair and wildness which spring up in the hearts of the poor when legal force, like a sharp harrow, goes over the most sensitive and vital rights of mankind. All this is contained in the land question. It is this which spreads through the people in three-fourths of Ireland with an all-pervading and thrilling intensity. It is this intolerable grief which has driven hundreds of thousands to America, there to bide the time of return. No greater self-deception could we practise on ourselves than to imagine that Fenianism is the folly of a few apprentices and shop-boys. Fenianism could not have survived for a year if it were not sustained by the traditional and just discontent of almost a whole people. Such acts of rashness and violence as have marked the last twelve months may be the work of a few, and those of no high or formidable classes ; but they would never have been perpetrated, they would never have been possible, if it were not for the profound estrangement of a large part of the people from British laws and from British Government. This feeling is to be found nowhere more calm, deep, and inflexible than among those who are in immediate contact with the 'land question,' that is, in the occupiers and tenants, and in the labourers, whose lot is better or worse as the occupiers and tenants prosper or are impoverished. These are neither apprentices nor shop-boys : neither are they a handful, but a population ; and a population in close kindred and living sympathy with millions who have tasted the civil and religious equality, and are thriving under the land laws, of the United States. Let us not deceive ourselves. Ireland is between two great assimilating powers, England and America. The play and action of America upon England, if it be seven days slower in reaching Ireland than that of England, is sevenfold

more penetrating and powerful upon the whole population. It is estimated that in the last twenty-five
years 24,000,000*l.* have been sent over by the Irish
in America for the relief or for the emigration of their
kindred and friends. The perfect unity of heart, will,
and purpose which unites the Irish on either side of
the Atlantic cannot be more complete. Add to this,
that the assimilating power of England, which has
overcome the resistance of Scotland, and absorbed it
into itself, is met by a stern repulsion in Ireland, which
keeps the two races asunder. Add again, that the
assimilating power of America is met and welcomed
with gratitude, sympathy, aspiration; that the atti-
tude of Ireland has long been, as Sir Robert Peel said
in Parliament five-and-twenty years ago:

With her back turned to England, and her face to the west.

Four millions and a half of Irish in Ireland turn
instinctively to five millions of Irish in America.

It is this that every statesman and citizen ought to
weigh; and the first condition to estimating the gravity
of the danger is to put away the childish shallowness
with which some of our public papers have treated
Fenianism. For nearly three hundred years, the same
diseases in Ireland have produced the same perils.
In the seventeenth century, the men who should have
been our strength were in the armies of Spain, Italy,
France, Germany, Poland, and the Low Countries.
In the eighteenth century, according to the records of
the War Office in France, 450,000 are stated to have
died between 1690 and 1745 in the French service;
and as many more, it is believed, between 1745 and

the beginning of this century. Is this imperial wisdom
or imperial strength ? My Lord, I will not pursue
these thoughts. I cannot think that the statesman
who will not staunch this ebbing of our life blood will
deserve well of his country. And I do not think that
any man who cannot, at least in some measure, do so
is a statesman. It needs little wisdom or capacity to
see that the constitution which fitted England, in its
childhood, when it was bounded by Berwick Castle and
the Cinque Ports, is a garment too narrow to cover
the limbs of three kingdoms. The Tudor Statutes
will not even clothe Great Britain. Presbyterian
Scotland has indignantly cast off the English Constitution in Church and State. Great Britain and Ireland
cannot any longer be straitened in the Penal Statutes
of Cromwell and the Revolution. We have outgrown
not only our swaddling clothes and the gear of our
childhood: we have become an empire of many races,
and of many religions; and the worst enemy of our
civil and religious peace could devise no surer policy
of discord, and no more fatal device of ruin, than
the attempt to keep alive the ascendency of race over
race, of religion over religion, of church over church.
A policy of absolute equality in religion is alone
imperial, and, I will add, if the empire is to hold
together, is alone possible. It is already, with few and
slight lingering imperfections, realised in our colonies
—Canada and Australia have led the way, and are
teaching the mother country how to live. I trust we
shall not be too proud to learn our lesson. As one
who towards the end of life can look back without
discerning a deed or word at variance with the heart-

felt loyalty of an Englishman, and as one who next after that which is not of this world desires earnestly to see maintained the unity, solidity, and prosperity of the British Empire, I implore all who are near the springs of sovereign power, and are able to guide by their wisdom the course of legislation, to take no rest until they shall have raised Ireland to an absolute equality, social, political, and religious, with England and Scotland, and shall have won back the love and fidelity of the noble-hearted, generous, heroic people of Catholic Ireland. Sir John Davies, Attorney-General in Ireland in 1613, no soft judge by nature or by office of the Irish nation, has left on record his opinion, formed on the experience of many years, ' That there is no nation of people under the sun that doth love equal and indifferent justice better than the Irish, or will rest better satisfied with the executions thereof, although it be against themselves, so that they may have the protection and benefits of the law when upon just cause they do desire it.'

Let 'equal and indifferent justice' be done even now, and the heart of Ireland may yet be won.

I have the honour to be,

My LORD,

Your obedient servant,

✠ H. E. MANNING.

March 12, 1868.

LONDON: PRINTED BY
SPOTTISWOODE AND CO., NEW-STREET SQUARE
AND PARLIAMENT STREET

www.ingramcontent.com/pod-product-compliance
Lightning Source LLC
Chambersburg PA
CBHW032138080426
42733CB00008B/1117